St. Louis Cardinals IQ: The Ultimate Test of True Fandom

Larry Underwood

IQ Series books are the trademark of Black Mesa Publishing, LLC.

Cataloging-in-Publication Data is available from the Library of Congress.

ISBN: 9780982675939
First edition, first printing.
Cover photo courtesy of Gloria Lee Dobbs.
Special thanks to Joel Katte.

Black Mesa Publishing, LLC
Florida
David Horne and Marc CB Maxwell
Black.Mesa.Publishing@gmail.com

www.blackmesabooks.com

Contents

Introduction

By Joel Katte
Author, Milwaukee Brewers IQ & County Stadium Kid

MANY PEOPLE LOVE TO HATE THE NEW YORK YANKEES. Well, I grew up hating the St. Louis Cardinals. In 1982, I was five and fell in love with baseball and the Milwaukee Brewers. It was the perfect year for a kid to fall in love with the Brewers. Well, almost perfect. Of course, I wish Game 7 of the World Series against the Cardinals had turned out differently … though you can be sure Larry Underwood, the author of this great book, was celebrating that night.

My dad grew up a Brooklyn Dodgers fan and my great Aunt Flo sent me Los Angeles Dodgers hats and shirts from California, so naturally my second favorite team was the Dodgers. Enduring the Ozzie Smith and Jack Clark home runs during the 1985 NLCS was brutal.

However, last summer after visiting the stunning city of St. Louis the week before the All-Star Game and after meeting lifelong Cardinals fanatic Larry Underwood, my hatred for the Redbirds turned to a sincere fondness. Walking down Elizabeth Street in "The Hill" and seeing where legendary catchers Joe Garagiola and Yogi Berra grew up next to each other seemed timeless. A grocery store clerk in the neighborhood told me the tale that Yogi and Joe played catch with each other from one side of the street to the other before they were old enough to cross the street. During my visit I noticed the Cardinals ballplayers and announcers immortalized in the city's "Walk of Fame" and slowly, I began to appreciate the Cardinals' culture and its historical significance for St. Louis and Major League Baseball.

Perhaps more impressive than the Cardinals Hall of Famers and their ten World Series titles are the dozens of one-of-a-kind nicknames like "Gas House Gang," "The Lip," "Vinegar Bend," "Dizzy," "Specs," "Country," and of course, "Ripper" and "The Ripper" to name a few. The nicknames seem to capture the essence of camaraderie shared by both players and fans and the stories and legacies that live on in memory.

In this book, Larry Underwood has compiled a fun read that Cardinals fans of all ages can enjoy. Embark on a journey through over 100-plus years of Cardinals history and keep score of all your "I was there when..." moments. With five chapters, 250 questions, and ten categories—The Numbers Game, The Rookies, The Veterans, The Legends, The Hitters, The Pitchers, The Managers, Coaches, Announcers, and Trades, The Fabulous Feats, The Teams, and Miscellaneous—the questions touch on every aspect of Cardinals' history. The chapters progress from Spring Training, to Opening Day, the All-Star Break, and the Dog Days of Summer, until finally you reach chapter five, and it is here that you will find out if you'll be playing October Baseball, and where you will be tested with trivia befitting a world champion. And it is here that legends are made—

this is your Cardinals IQ, The Ultimate Test of True Fandom.

Good Luck!

Chapter One

SPRING TRAINING

THIS IS SPRING TRAINING MIND YOU. We're only stretching here. Just trying to get limber after a long winter of chips, couches, remote controls, beverages of choice, and the NFL ... I mean, there's no sense straining a groin or anything else right out of the box. So we'll just start with some basics – a few Cardinals legends and some numbers that go with them.

No point in sweating bullets over these questions. You don't know these, well, you don't know Jack (Buck?). Or Mike Shannon for that matter!

THE NUMBERS GAME

QUESTION 1: Stan Musial had 3,630 hits in his career. What was unusual about that total?
  a) He played the harmonica 3,630 times in the clubhouse after the games, as well
  b) He gave 3,630 post game interviews to Harry Caray
  c) Exactly half of his hits were at home, and half on the road
  d) He once used his harmonica to record one of his hits and the record went platinum.

QUESTION 2: How many home runs did Stan Musial hit during his career?
  a)   475
  b)   363
  c)   501
  d)   490

QUESTION 3: What number did Dizzy Dean wear while playing for the Cardinals?
  a)   47
  b)   37
  c)   17
  d)   27

QUESTION 4: In 1967, the Cardinals got off to a fast start, winning how many games in a row, before finally losing one?
  a)   9
  b)   6
  c)   11
  d)   8

QUESTION 5: In 1979, Keith Hernandez led the National League in batting and was named co-MVP. What was his batting average that season?
  a)   .341
  b)   .356
  c)   .323
  d)   .344

THE ROOKIES

QUESTION 6: Nicknamed "The Fulton Flash," he was once named the National League Rookie of the Year.
- a) Ted Sizemore
- b) Bill Virdon
- c) Bake McBride
- d) Wally Moon

QUESTION 7: This rookie pitcher won 16 games for the Cardinals in 1967.
- a) Steve Carlton
- b) Dick Hughes
- c) Nelson Briles
- d) Reggie Cleveland

QUESTION 8: This rookie first baseman was a disappointment for the Cardinals in 1970.
- a) Joe Hague
- b) Keith Hernandez
- c) Jose Cruz
- d) Reggie Smith

QUESTION 9: This slick fielding third baseman broke in with the Cardinals in 1972, hitting .359 in 21 games.
- a) Hector Cruz
- b) Ken Reitz
- c) Norman Mailer
- d) Gene Simmons

QUESTION 10: This rookie catcher once got four hits in a single World Series game.
   a) Branch Rickey
   b) Joe Garagiola
   c) Tom Nieto
   d) Jose Molina

THE VETERANS

QUESTION 11: This backup catcher helped the Cardinals win the World Series in 1982.
   a) Steve Lake
   b) Gene Tenace
   c) Tom Nieto
   d) Dave Ricketts

QUESTION 12: In the final inning of the 1985 NLCS, Dodger manager Tom Lasorda elected to pitch to this Cardinals slugger, with first base open and Andy Van Slyke on deck.
   a) David Green
   b) Bob Horner
   c) Jack Clark
   d) Pedro Guerrero

QUESTION 13: This Whitey Herzog early free agent acquisition was a bust during the regular season, but a two-time MVP in the postseason.
   a) George Hendrick
   b) Tom Lawless
   c) Darryl Porter
   d) Tom Pagnozzi

QUESTION 14: This consistent third baseman once hit exactly 24 home runs per season for four consecutive seasons.
   a) Ken Reitz
   b) Joe Torre
   c) Ken Boyer
   d) Mike Shannon

QUESTION 15: This slugger was traded to the Dodgers for Ted Sizemore.
   a) Reggie Smith
   b) Dick Allen
   c) Art Shamsky
   d) Pedro Guerrero

Note: Spring Training is gearing up for the regular season. No more, easy "multiple choice" questions!

THE LEGENDS

QUESTION 16: Who was the last National League player to win the Triple Crown?

QUESTION 17: Who did Nelson Briles replace in the starting rotation after a broken leg suffered on July 15, 1967 put him on the disabled list for eight weeks?

QUESTION 18: What player was nearly traded to the Philadelphia Phillies for pitcher Robin Roberts in 1958?

QUESTION 19: Whose home run in the bottom of the 12th gave the National League a 6-5 victory over the American League in the 1955 All-Star Game at Milwaukee's County Stadium?

QUESTION 20: With the Cardinals trailing the Yankees in the World Series 2 games to 1, and down 3-0 in the game, his grand slam home run turned the tide for the Cardinals in the 1964 World Series. Who hit this clutch home run?

THE HITTERS

QUESTION 21: What player's .358 lifetime batting average is second only to Ty Cobb's .367?

QUESTION 22: This power hitting first baseman's nickname was "The Big Cat." Name him.

QUESTION 23: Who's the only player in Major League history to have two grand slam home runs in the same inning, off the same pitcher, no less?

QUESTION 24: Despite hitting fewer than ten home runs in 1985, this clutch hitter drove in 110 runs for the pennant-winning Cardinals in 1985.

QUESTION 25: This legendary game-winning grand slam gave the Cardinals an extra-inning 7-6 victory over Houston, on May 1, 1979. Who hit it?

THE PITCHERS

QUESTION 26: A World Series hero in 1982, this pitcher's temper tantrum in Game 7 of the 1985 World Series was directed towards home plate umpire Don Denkinger. Who was this hot head?

QUESTION 27: This rookie pitcher won Game 6 of the 1982 World Series for the Cardinals. Who was he?

QUESTION 28: Name the 24-year-old right-hander who led the National League with a 2.52 earned run average in 1976.

QUESTION 29: Name the left-handed pitcher who won 20 games for the World Champion Cardinals in 1964.

QUESTION 30: Name the left-hander who was the losing pitcher in Game 7 of the 1985 World Series debacle against Kansas City.

THE MANAGERS, COACHES, ANNOUNCERS, AND TRADES

QUESTION 31: Bing Devine's first player acquisition brought this Cardinal great to the team from the Cincinnati Reds in 1958.

QUESTION 32: This power hitting first baseman was acquired from the San Francisco Giants for pitcher Sam Jones in 1959.

QUESTION 33: He struck out in his first at bat as a Cardinal, after joining the team on June 15, 1964; who was he?

QUESTION 34: Which Cardinal great cried like a baby after being traded to the Yankees prior to the start of the1954 season?

QUESTION 35: His attempt to discipline the team by forbidding facial hair during the 1978 season, led to his early dismissal as manager. Who was it?

THE FABULOUS FEATS

QUESTION 36: Who stole a rookie National League record 110 bases in 1985?

QUESTION 37: His surprising steal of home in 1982 helped spur the Cardinals on to a division title, and subsequent World Series championship.

QUESTION 38: In a call immortalized by Harry Caray, this Cardinals base runner scored from first on a single to center by Roger Maris when the centerfielder bobbled the ball. The run propelled the Cardinals to a thrilling August 1967 win over the Chicago Cubs at Busch Stadium. Who was this daring base runner?

QUESTION 39: This switch-hitter is the only player to ever record at least 100 hits from both sides of the plate in one season.

QUESTION 40: Who hit .478 for the Cards in the '64 World Series seven-game victory over the New York Yankees?

THE TEAMS

QUESTION 41: When was the last time a Cardinals team ever finished last in the standings?

QUESTION 42: In 1985, the Cardinals began the regular season losing how many games in a row?

QUESTION 43: True or false: The Cardinals have never won back-to-back World Series championships.

QUESTION 44: Until the Boston Red Sox swept the Cardinals in the 2004 World Series, how many consecutive World Series appearances did the Cards extend to a full seven games?

QUESTION 45: How many times in postseason history have the Cards blown 3 games to 1 leads, establishing a dubious record for futility?

MISCELLANEOUS

QUESTION 46: Name the Cardinals player who coined, "El Birdos" as the team's nickname in the late '60s?

QUESTION 47: In what year did every Cardinals regular bat over .300?

QUESTION 48: How many times did Lou Brock steal home during his career?

QUESTION 49: Whose rare fielding miscue late in Game 7 cost the Cardinals the 1968 World Series?

QUESTION 50: Name the two teams Bob Forsch no-hit during his career.

Chapter One Answer Key

Time to find out how you did – put a check mark next to the questions you answered correctly, and when you are done be sure to add up you score to find out your IQ, and to find out if you made the Opening Day roster!

THE NUMBERS GAME

___**QUESTION 1:** C – Musial was the model of consistency during his career, spreading his hits evenly between home and away games – 1,815 apiece.

___**QUESTION 2:** A – Musial had 475 career home runs.

___**QUESTION 3:** C – Dizzy Dean wore number 17.

___**QUESTION 4:** B – The Cards won their first six games in 1967.

___**QUESTION 5:** D – Hernandez hit .344 in 1979.

THE ROOKIES

___**QUESTION 6:** C – Bake McBride was nicknamed "The Fulton Flash" by broadcaster Mike Shannon, en route to winning the 1974 NL Rookie of the Year award.

___**QUESTION 7:** B – Dick Hughes won 16 games for the Cardinals as a 29-year-old rookie in 1967. The following season, an arm injury ended his brief career.

___**QUESTION 8:** A – The Cardinals were expecting big things from their rookie first baseman in 1970, but Joe Hague was a disappointment, with only 14 home runs.

___**QUESTION 9:** B – Ken Reitz hit an impressive .359 in limited play in 1972. That was a fluke for one of the slowest players in the history of the game.

___**QUESTION 10:** B – Rookie catcher Joe Garagiola banged out four hits in Game 3 of the 1946 World Series. Meanwhile, Joe's neighborhood pal Yogi Berra was embarking on a Hall of Fame career with the New York Yankees. They just had to sign Garagiola?

THE VETERANS

___**QUESTION 11:** B – Ten years after starring in the '72 World Series for Oakland, Gene Tenace provided much needed bench support in helping the Cards reach the Promised Land in '82.

___**QUESTION 12:** C – Jack Clark wasn't called "Jack the Ripper" for nothing, as he ripped a first pitch fastball over the left field fence for a pennant-clinching home run in '85, against a poorly managed Dodger team.

___QUESTION 13: C – Darryl Porter didn't have much to write home about during the regular season, but his bat came alive in the postseason to help the Cards win the '82 World Series over the Milwaukee Brewers.

___QUESTION 14: C – Ken Boyer had pretty good power and won a NL MVP award in '64, helping the Cards win the World Series, but his consistency was remarkable; 24 home runs for four consecutive years in the '60s!

___QUESTION 15: B – After the '69 season, the Cards figured they needed some power, so they acquired Dick Allen from the Phillies; he responded with 34 home runs and 101 runs batted in. Naturally, the front office then decided they didn't need all that power after all, and traded him for a singles hitter – Ted Sizemore, after the season ended.

THE LEGENDS

___QUESTION 16: Albert Pujols hasn't quite done it yet; but he probably will win the Triple Crown before his career is over. As it stands right now, the last NL player to accomplish that feat is none other than Joe "Ducky" Medwick, way back in 1937.

___QUESTION 17: In July of '67, Roberto Clemente hit a vicious line drive off Bob Gibson's right leg, causing a slight fracture just below the knee cap. Gibson would be shelved for a couple of months, but came back stronger than ever to power the Cardinals past the Red Sox in the World Series. In the meantime, Nelson Briles stepped into the starting rotation after Gibby went down, and pitched brilliantly, proving to be a rising star.

___QUESTION 18: While Frank Lane was the Cardinals' General Manager back in the late '50s, he tried to swing a deal which would send Stan Musial to Philadelphia, in exchange for pitcher Robin Roberts. Ownership vetoed the deal, and "Trader Lane" was sent packing, shortly thereafter.

___QUESTION 19: Speak of the Devil! It was none other than Stan Musial who hit the dramatic, game-winning home run in the '55 All-Star Game in Milwaukee.

___QUESTION 20: Ken Boyer was the hero in Game 4 of the '64 World Series. Boyer's blast, a dramatic grand slam home run off Yankees pitcher Al Downing, turned a 3-0 deficit into a 4-3 victory.

THE HITTERS

___QUESTION 21: Rogers Hornsby, who played for the Cardinals from 1915 to 1926, and then again briefly in 1933, recorded the second highest lifetime batting average of all-time. With his .358 mark, only Cobb was better.

___QUESTION 22: This is a tricky one. Andres Gallaraga spent one injury plagued season with the Cardinals (1992) before heading to the hitter friendly confines of Coors Field; but his nickname was "The Cat"; not "The Big Cat"; that nickname belonged to Hall of Fame slugger Johnny Mize, who played for the Cardinals from 1936 to 1941. If you got that one correct, you're probably going to go far in this league!

___QUESTION 23: Free-swinging third baseman Fernando Tatis is the only player in MLB history to hit two grand slam home runs in the same inning; and he'll probably be the only one to do it for the next 1,000 years or so. As a footnote to this amazing feat, Tatis connected off the same pitcher for both big blows – Chan Ho Park – who probably wishes he would've been pulled after the first third-inning dinger! The date of this historic performance: April 23, 1999. The location: Dodger Stadium.

___QUESTION 24: In 1985, second baseman Tom Herr accomplished the rare feat of driving in over 100 runs in a season (110), without making it to double digits in home runs (8). With guys like Vince Coleman and Willie McGee always on base, and frequently in scoring position, all Tommy had to do was hit a line drive somewhere; he did, with great proficiency!

___QUESTION 25: Pinch-hitter Roger Freed connected on a 3-2 fastball thrown by Houston reliever Joe Sambito with two outs and the bases loaded in the bottom of the 11th inning; turning a 6-3 deficit into a stunning 7-6 Cardinals win.

THE PITCHERS

___**QUESTION 26:** Joaquin Andujar, taking his frustration out on Don Denkinger, whose bad call at first base the night before helped the Royals win, complained bitterly on every close call that didn't go his way. It didn't matter as the Royals blew the Cardinals out in Game 7 of the '85 World Series, 11-0.

___**QUESTION 27:** John Stupor stupefied the Milwaukee Brewers in Game 6 of the 1982 World Series, as the Cardinals won, 13-1, forcing a deciding Game 7.

___**QUESTION 28:** John Denny led the NL with that 2.52 earned run average in 1976, but still only managed to win 11 games that year, for a less than stellar Redbird edition.

___**QUESTION 29:** A young and talented Ray Sadecki won 20 games for the Cardinals in 1964, as the team won its first World Series championship since 1946.

___**QUESTION 30:** John Tudor was sensational throughout the 1985 campaign, but came up empty in the big game, getting clobbered by a fired up Royals team in Game 7 of the World Series.

THE MANAGERS, COACHES, ANNOUNCERS, AND TRADES

___QUESTION 31: Curt Flood came to the Cardinals as an erratic third baseman from the Cincinnati Reds in 1957. He was converted to centerfield and became a star.

___QUESTION 32: Bing Devine pulled off another great trade the following year, bringing perennial All-Star first baseman Bill White over from the San Francisco Giants.

___QUESTION 33: Lou Brock got off to a shaky start for his new team, striking out in his first at bat as a Cardinal, against Houston.

___QUESTION 34: Enos Slaughter loved playing for the Cardinals, and even a trade to the mighty Yankees didn't console him.

___QUESTION 35: Vern Rapp learned the hard way that worrying about silly things like haircuts and facial hair don't win games and sure don't make the players happy.

THE FABULOUS FEATS

___QUESTION 36: Nicknamed "Vincent Van Go," rookie speedster Vince Coleman swiped a Major League rookie record 110 bases in 1985. Ironically, in the postseason, a tarp traveling at three miles per hour caught him and put him on the bench for the World Series.

___**QUESTION 37:** Backup catcher Glenn Brummer surprised everybody when he stole home with two outs and two strikes on the batter, David Green, in the bottom of the ninth inning in a tie game against the San Francisco Giants. The dramatic win came at a time when the Cardinals were struggling to take command of the division race; that one play gave them much needed momentum for the stretch run.

___**QUESTION 38:** Back in August of '67, when the Cards were battling the Cubs for the pennant, Curt Flood streaked all the way around from first base on a Roger Maris ninth inning single to center to give the Cards a big win against Chicago. The Cards went on to sweep that series at Busch Stadium, and the Cubbies were all but dead. In case you were wondering, centerfielder Ted Savage bobbled Maris' hit, just enough to give Flood the chance to score the run.

___**QUESTION 39:** Switch-hitting Gary Templeton is the only player in MLB history to collect over 100 hits from both sides of the plate in a single season (1979). The Cards were notoriously weak, as a team, versus left-handed pitchers that season; that's why Templeton had so many opportunities as a right-handed batter.

___**QUESTION 40:** Tim McCarver hit a robust .478 in the 1964 World Series against the Yankees. His battery mate, Bob Gibson, aced him out as the Series MVP, however.

THE TEAMS

__Question 41: Only three years removed from a trip to the World Series, the 1990 edition of the Cardinals had a disastrous season, finishing last in the NL East; Whitey Herzog must've sensed the inevitable and resigned shortly before the All-Star break.

__Question 42: The experts predicted the Cards would finish dead last in 1985. After losing their first four games of the season, it seemed they were headed for the cellar. Wrong! They won 101 games and finished first in the NL East.

__Question 43: They nearly pulled it off in '67-'68; but the Cards have never won back-to-back World Series championships.

__Question 44: Before being swept by the Red Sox in 2004, the Cards had played in seven consecutive seven-game World Series contests: 1946, 1964, 1967, 1968, 1982, 1985, and 1987.

__Question 45: The Cards have the dubious distinction of being the only team to blow three separate 3 games to 1 leads in the postseason: 1968 against the Detroit Tigers, 1985 against the Kansas City Royals, and 1996 against the Atlanta Braves (NLCS).

MISCELLANEOUS

___**QUESTION 46:** During the '67 season, Orlando Cepeda usually led the post game celebrations with his rallying cry, "Bravo, bravo, El Birdos!"

___**QUESTION 47:** If 1968 was "The Year of the Pitcher," 1930 was definitely "The Year of the Hitter," as every Cardinal regular chipped in with at least a .300 batting average.

___**QUESTION 48:** Believe it or not, Glenn Brummer, with one career steal of home, ranks ahead of Lou Brock in that department, who never stole home.

___**QUESTION 49:** Curt Flood broke in when Jim Northrup lined a shot to straight away center, then slipped as he tried to break back on the ball, which sailed over his head for a two-run triple, as the Tigers beat the Cardinals, 4-1, in Game 7 of the '68 World Series.

___**QUESTION 50:** Bob Forsch tossed two no-hitters in his career. His first one came at Busch Stadium against the Philadelphia Phillies (1978) and his second was on the road against the Montreal Expos (1984).

Got your Spring Training total? Here's how it breaks down:

A Fantasy League Master	= 45-50
Opening Day Starter	= 40-44
You're A Big Leaguer	= 35-39
Utility Player At Best	= 30-34
Another Season In The Minors	= 00-29

The easy part is behind us—now it's time to experience the pressure of the Major Leagues. Good luck on Opening Day!

Chapter Two

OPENING DAY

YOU'VE MADE THE ROSTER and you're looking forward to helping your team make the postseason—maybe even win the World Series. It's time to hone your skills in preparation for big league action. The categories stay the same, but it gets more intense. We're about to find out whether or not you can play this game for the long haul. Let's play ball!

THE NUMBERS GAME

QUESTION 51: Name the player who hit a paltry .103 in the '67 World Series for the Cardinals.

QUESTION 52: Name the player who hit a similarly paltry .111 in the '64 World Series for the Cardinals.

QUESTION 53: Name the unsung pitching hero for the '64 Cardinals who gave up no runs in five innings of work, striking out nine and securing a crucial World Series victory.

QUESTION 54: How many games did the Dean Brothers combine to win in 1934?

QUESTION 55: Who led the team with 98 runs batted in during the 1942 regular season, as the

Cards went 106-48, en route to a World Series championship?

THE ROOKIES

QUESTION 56: Whose two home runs in Game 3 of the '82 World Series stunned the baseball world?

QUESTION 57: This brother of a Cardinal legend won seven games as a rookie pitcher in 1950. Who was he?

QUESTION 58: Who won 20 games for the Cardinals as a rookie pitcher in 1953?

QUESTION 59: Who was the NL Rookie of the Year in 1954?

QUESTION 60: Who was the NL Rookie of the Year in 1955?

THE VETERANS

QUESTION 61: Playing in his second World Series, this veteran went 2 for 3 as a pinch-hitter in the 1964 World Series.

QUESTION 62: Whose six runs batted in for the Cardinals led the team in the '64 World Series?

QUESTION 63: Who called it quits after hitting .158 for the Cardinals in the '68 World Series?

QUESTION 64: This former All-Star helped the Cardinals down the stretch in 1985, frequently filling in for an injured Jack Clark, while batting well over .400. Who was this key late-season acquisition?

QUESTION 65: Acquired in a trade from the White Sox, he played in just 39 games with the Cardinals in 1962, hitting under .200. Who was he?

THE LEGENDS

QUESTION 66: Whose home run off Giants pitcher Juan Marichal, drove in the first runs of the season for the Cards, in 1967?

QUESTION 67: In his only full season with the Cardinals, this Hall of Fame shortstop played for the 1928 pennant-winning team, before being traded. Who was he?

QUESTION 68: He played in 46 games for the Cardinals in 1933, hitting a solid .325, before being traded to the Browns, where he finished his career. Who was he?

QUESTION 69: This trio was dubbed "the fastest outfield ever" in a 1969 edition of *Sporting News*. Name them.

QUESTION 70: Whose dramatic home run off Johnny Podres tied a crucial late September 1963 game for the Cardinals? It was also the last homer of his career.

The Hitters

Question 71: Who finished second to Bill Madlock in the NL batting race in 1975?

Question 72: Who was the last National Leaguer to hit over .370?

Question 73: Who hit the first Major League grand slam home run in Canada?

Question 74: What was Ken Boyer's longest hitting streak?

Question 75: Who holds the Major League record for most hits in one season by a catcher?

The Pitchers

Question 76: How many times did Bob Gibson win at least 20 games?

Question 77: What Hall of Fame pitcher was traded by the Cardinals after his rookie season and went on to win 20 games for six straight years?

Question 78: What Cardinals pitcher tossed shutouts in both the 1930 and 1931 World Series?

QUESTION 79: Who struck out the first five hitters he faced in Game 5 of the 1943 World Series vs. the New York Yankees?

QUESTION 80: What Cardinals pitcher gave up World Series home runs to Carl Yastrzemski, Reggie Smith and Rico Petrocelli – *in the same inning*?

THE MANAGERS, COACHES, ANNOUNCERS, AND TRADES

QUESTION 81: Who did the Cardinals trade to acquire Willie McGee?

QUESTION 82: What managing milestone did Whitey Herzog achieve in 1987?

QUESTION 83: Why did Tony LaRussa choose to wear number 10 on his uniform?

QUESTION 84: How many seasons did Red Schoendienst manage the Cardinals?

QUESTION 85: Name the only Cardinals manager to win three pennants in a row.

THE FABULOUS FEATS

QUESTION 86: During the 1940s, St. Louis Cardinals players won three straight MVP awards. Name them and the years they accomplished the feat.

QUESTION 87: Which three Cardinals won MVP awards in the '60s?

QUESTION 88: Which three Cardinals won MVP awards in the '30s?

QUESTION 89: In what year did the Cardinals draw two million fans for the first time?

QUESTION 90: In what years did Stan Musial win Most Valuable Player awards?

THE TEAMS

QUESTION 91: In what years did the Cardinals consecutively win 106, 105, and 105 games?

QUESTION 92: When were the Cardinals officially given their name?

QUESTION 93: When did the team first occupy Sportsman's Park?

QUESTION 94: What year did the Cardinals play their first night game in St. Louis?

QUESTION 95: What year did the Cards play the St. Louis Browns in the World Series?

MISCELLANEOUS

QUESTION 96: How many consecutive seasons did Lou Brock steal 50 or more bases?

QUESTION 97: Who had 24 pinch-hits for the Cardinals in 1970?

QUESTION 98: Aside from Mark McGwire, name two other Cardinals who wore number 25 since 1960.

QUESTION 99: What Cardinals player set a Major League record by hitting three home runs in his first two games ever played?

QUESTION 100: Who led the National League with 13 triples in 1966?

Chapter Two Answer Key

Time to find out how you did – put a check mark next to the questions you answered correctly, and when you're done be sure to add up your score to find out your IQ, and to find out if you deserve a shot a the Mid-Summer Classic.

THE NUMBERS GAME

___**QUESTION 51:** Orlando Cepeda was the NL MVP in '67, but he was a flop in the World Series, hitting a mere .103.

___**QUESTION 52:** Bill White had a solid regular season, but only managed to hit .111 in the '64 World Series against the Yankees.

___**QUESTION 53:** Roger Craig came out of the bullpen to save Game 4 of the '64 World Series against the Yankees, with the help of Ken Boyer's dramatic grand slam home run.

___**QUESTION 54:** Old Diz won 30 and brother, Paul, won 19 games for the '34 Gashouse Gang. That comes to 49, podnuh.

___**QUESTION 55:** Enos "Country" Slaughter didn't quite reach the century mark, but his 98 runs batted in led the '42 Cards, en route to a World Series championship.

THE ROOKIES

___**QUESTION 56:** Willie McGee hit two home runs and made two great plays in centerfield in Game 3 to help the Cards take command of the '82 World Series.

___**QUESTION 57:** Cloyd Boyer preceded his brother Ken to the Cardinals, winning seven games as a rookie pitcher in 1952.

___**QUESTION 58:** Harvey Haddix had a tremendous rookie year for the Cards in 1953, piling up 20 wins.

___**QUESTION 59:** Wally Moon hit over .300 and scored over 100 runs, en route to the 1954 Rookie of the Year award.

___**QUESTION 60:** Bill Virdon hit a solid .281 with 17 home runs in 1955, en route to his Rookie of the Year award.

THE VETERANS

___**QUESTION 61:** Bob Skinner, who also played for the World Champion Pittsburgh Pirates in 1960, chipped in with a couple of pinch-hits in three at bats in '64.

___**QUESTION 62:** Ken Boyer led the Cardinals with six RBIs in the '64 World Series.

___**QUESTION 63:** Roger Maris said "goodbye" to baseball after the '68 season, and "hello" to a beer distributorship, compliments of August Busch.

___**QUESTION 64:** César Cedeño provided the Cards with the power they needed after slugger Jack Clark went down with a late-season injury in '85.

___**QUESTION 65:** At the age of 40, Minnie Minoso was hurt early and often during a bad '62 season and was sent packing the following year.

THE LEGENDS

___**QUESTION 66:** With two men on base, Lou Brock's dramatic Opening Day home run off Giants ace Juan Marichal propelled the Cards to a 6-0 victory.

___**QUESTION 67:** Rabbit Maranville stopped by for nine games in 1927 and 112 games in 1928 before scurrying off to the Boston Braves the following year.

___**QUESTION 68:** Rogers Hornsby made that final curtain call for the Cardinals in 1933, proving he could still hit a little bit at the age of 37.

___**QUESTION 69:** Just before the start of the '69 season, Lou Brock, Curt Flood and Vada Pinson were featured on the cover of *Sporting News*, but the "fastest outfield ever" was quickly slowed down by injuries to Pinson and Flood.

___**QUESTION 70:** In his last hurrah, Stan Musial hit career home run number 475 in a late-season game against the Dodgers in 1963, but it wasn't enough as the Dodgers swept the three-game series in St. Louis. The Cards would have to wait 'til next year to win it all, with a new left fielder by the name of Brock.

THE HITTERS

___**QUESTION 71:** Ted Simmons hit a solid .332 in 1975, finishing second in the batting race behind Bill Madlock's .354.

___**QUESTION 72:** Stan Musial led the NL in 1948 with an impressive .376 batting average; no other NL player has hit over .370 since.

___**QUESTION 73:** On Opening Day in 1969, at Montreal's Jarry Park, Dal Maxvill lofted a lazy fly ball to right field and wound up with a wind blown grand slam home run, the first ever regular season grand slam home run hit outside the United States.

___**QUESTION 74:** Boyer's longest hitting streak was 29 games in 1959.

___**QUESTION 75:** Ted Simmons had 193 hits in 1975 to establish a ML record for catchers.

THE PITCHERS

___QUESTION 76: Gibson was a 20-game winner five times.

___QUESTION 77: Three-Finger Brown was traded to the Cubs after his rookie year (1903), and went on to win 20 games for six consecutive seasons: 1906-11.

___QUESTION 78: Wild Bill Hallahan pitched shutouts for the Redbirds in both the 1930 and 1931 World Series.

___QUESTION 79: Mort Cooper struck out the first five batters he faced in Game 5 of the 1943 World Series, but he got no run support, as the Cards lost the game, 2-0; not to mention the Series, 4 games to 1.

___QUESTION 80: Rookie pitcher Dick Hughes gave up the three long balls in the fourth inning of Game 6 in 1967 against Boston; but we all know what happened in Game 7, don't we?

THE MANAGERS, COACHES, ANNOUNCERS, AND TRADES

___QUESTION 81: The Cards traded left-handed pitcher Bob Sykes to the Yankees in exchange for prospect Willie McGee.

___**QUESTION 82:** In addition to guiding his team to the World Series in 1987, Herzog also won his 1,000th career regular season game that year.

___**QUESTION 83:** Tony LaRussa chose to wear the number 10 on his jersey because his goal was to win the tenth World Series championship for the Cardinals franchise; he did it in 2006.

___**QUESTION 84:** Red Schoendienst managed the Cardinals for 13 different seasons.

___**QUESTION 85:** Billy Southworth is the first and only Cardinals manager to win three consecutive NL pennants for the franchise (1942-44).

THE FABULOUS FEATS

___**QUESTION 86:** Mort Cooper (1942), Stan Musial (1943), and Marty Marion (1944) won three straight MVP awards for the Cardinals.

___**QUESTION 87:** Ken Boyer (1964), Orlando Cepeda (1967), and Bob Gibson (1968) won MVP awards in the '60s for the Cardinals.

___**QUESTION 88:** Frankie Frisch (1931), Dizzy Dean (1934), and Joe Medwick (1937) won MVP awards in the '30s for the Cardinals.

___**QUESTION 89:** The Cardinals first drew 2 million fans during the 1967 season.

___QUESTION 90: Musial won the MVP award in 1943, 1946, and 1948.

THE TEAMS

___QUESTION 91: The Cardinals won all those games in 1942, 1943, and 1944.

___QUESTION 92: The Cardinals officially got their name prior to the start of the 1899 season.

___QUESTION 93: The Cardinals first played in Sportsman's Park during the 1920 season.

___QUESTION 94: The Cardinals first home night game was in 1940.

___QUESTION 95: Dubbed "The Streetcar Series" the Cardinals and the Browns faced off in the 1944 World Series.

MISCELLANEOUS

___QUESTION 96: Lou Brock stole 50 or more bases for 12 consecutive seasons (1965-76).

___QUESTION 97: Vic Davalillo had 24 pinch-hits for the Cards in 1970.

___QUESTION 98: Both Julian Javier and George Hendrick wore number 25 for the Cardinals, along with Big Mac.

___**QUESTION 99:** Joe Cunningham performed the feat in 1954.

___**QUESTION 100:** Tim McCarver not only led the NL with 13 triples in 1966. He also established a record for most triples hit by a catcher in a season.

How was your Opening Day performance? Add up the totals and find out if you're a contender or pretender. Here's the breakdown:

THE SECOND COMING OF ALBERT PUJOLS	= 45-50
THE FANS LOVE YOU	= 40-44
YOU'RE A SOLID PLAYER	= 35-39
PART-TIME PLAYER	= 30-34
BACK TO THE MINORS, KID	= 00-29

Good luck becoming an All-Star!

Chapter Three

ALL-STAR

SO DO YOU THINK YOU'VE GOT WHAT IT TAKES to be an All-Star? For starters, you've got to bring your "A" game to the field every day, and you've got to be better than anyone else, as well. At this stage of the game, you either have what it takes to intimidate the competition, or you fall by the wayside. This is no place for wimps; let's see if you qualify to be one of the game's elite—an All-Star. Good luck!

THE NUMBERS GAME

QUESTION 101: When the Cardinals won the NL pennant in 1964, what teams finished second and third?

QUESTION 102: In what season did the Cardinals lead the NL with a 2.49 team earned run average?

QUESTION 103: In what season did the Cardinals lead the NL with 1,004 runs scored?

QUESTION 104: In what season did the Cardinals win the World Series despite finishing last in home runs in the National League?

QUESTION 105: In what season did the Cardinals steal 304 bases (fourth highest total in ML history)?

THE ROOKIES

QUESTION 106: Name the four Cardinal outfielders to win Rookie of the Year awards.

QUESTION 107: Name the rookie outfielder who hit .373 for the 1930 Cardinals.

QUESTION 108: Name the rookie who was called up due to an injury to Willie McGee.

QUESTION 109: Name the rookie who was called up due to an injury to David Green.

QUESTION 110: Name the rookie Howard Cosell said "looks like 'ET'!"

THE VETERANS

QUESTION 111: Name the Hall of Fame pitcher whose last victory came with the Cardinals in 1929.

QUESTION 112: Name the player whose last regular season hit in 1968 was a triple, before retiring.

QUESTION 113: Name the former American League pitching star who helped stabilize the Cardinals' pitching staff during its 1982 championship season.

QUESTION 114: What Hall of Fame pitcher was nicknamed "Ol' Stubblebeard?"

QUESTION 115: What pitcher surrendered Stan Musial's 3,000th hit, before joining the Cardinals over a decade later?

THE LEGENDS

QUESTION 116: Name the Cardinals pitcher who briefly played for the Harlem Globetrotters.

QUESTION 117: What was Hall of Fame pitcher Grover Alexander's nickname?

QUESTION 118: Name the only brothers to start as pitcher and catcher in the All-Star Game.

QUESTION 119: How many times did Rogers Hornsby win the batting championship?

QUESTION 120: What year did the entire Cardinals infield start in the All-Star Game?

THE HITTERS

QUESTION 121: Who holds the National League record for doubles (64) in a season?

QUESTION 122: Who hit the first home run in the 2006 World Series?

QUESTION 123: Whose home run on September 8, 1998 proved to be the shortest one he'd hit all year?

QUESTION 124: Whose first career home run in 1985 also happened to be an inside-the-park job?

QUESTION 125: What was the outcome of the doubleheader played between the Cardinals and Giants, when Stan Musial connected for a record setting five home runs?

THE PITCHERS

QUESTION 126: Name the pitcher who set a NL record with 45 saves in 1984.

QUESTION 127: Name the only pitcher other than Bob Gibson to record a win in the 1967 World Series.

QUESTION 128: Who was a 21-game winner for the Cardinals at the age of 40?

QUESTION 129: Name the pitcher who was nicknamed "Double Cheeseburger."

QUESTION 130: How many times was Bob Gibson knocked out of a game in 1968, before retiring the side?

THE MANAGERS, COACHES, ANNOUNCERS, AND TRADES

QUESTION 131: Name the Cardinals announcer whose first job in broadcasting was doing play-by-play for the Ohio State Buckeyes football team.

QUESTION 132: Name the two teams Harry Caray did play-by-play for after getting fired from the Cardinals and before getting hired by the Cubs.

QUESTION 133: Who did the Cardinals acquire from Philadelphia after the 1971 season in exchange for Steve Carlton?

QUESTION 134: Whose three-run home run in Game 7 of the 1987 NLCS propelled the Cardinals to victory?

QUESTION 135: Name the Cardinals infielder who broke in with two 100 RBI seasons in the 1950s before being traded.

THE FABULOUS FEATS

QUESTION 136: Name the only player to hit four home runs and drive in 12 runs in the same game.

QUESTION 137: Who was the first player to ever record 12 RBIs in a single game?

QUESTION 138: Name the Cardinals player to hit for the cycle in a losing cause against the Chicago Cubs in a June 1984 extra-inning game at Wrigley Field.

QUESTION 139: Name the only player to ever hit a ball (foul) out of old Busch Stadium.

QUESTION 140: Name the player who scored from first base on George Hendrick's double down the left field line, on Opening Day 1980. It was the only run scored in the game, as the Cards temporarily tamed the World Champion Pittsburgh Pirates.

THE TEAMS

QUESTION 141: When Mark McGwire hit 70 home runs in 1998, who were the other three players on the team with at least 25 home runs that year?

QUESTION 142: When was the last time the Cardinals had three outfielders with enough at bats to qualify for the batting title to all hit over .300 in a single season?

QUESTION 143: Name the Cardinals third baseman who led the team with 26 errors while hitting a miserable .228 that season.

QUESTION 144: Excluding strike years, what Cards team is the last ML squad to hit fewer than 60 home runs in a single season?

QUESTION 145: When did the Cardinals finish exactly a game and a half behind the division champions in back-to-back seasons?

MISCELLANEOUS

QUESTION 146: True or False: Albert Pujols has scored at least 100 runs in each of the nine seasons he's played in the Major Leagues.

QUESTION 147: True or False: Albert Pujols has driven in at least 100 runs in each of the nine seasons he's played in the Major Leagues.

QUESTION 148: True or False: After nine seasons in the Major Leagues, Albert Pujols has a higher lifetime batting average than Stan Musial.

QUESTION 149: What Cardinals player was nicknamed "The Lip?"

QUESTION 150: Name the only two players who were with the Cardinals in 1980 and 1987.

Chapter Three Answer Key

Time to find out how you did – put a check mark next to the questions you answered correctly, and when you're done be sure to add up your score to find out your IQ, whether or not you're an All-Star, and to find out if you have a shot at making the postseason. The race is heating up—good luck!

THE NUMBERS GAME

___**QUESTION 101:** In 1964, the Cards finished a game ahead of both the Philadelphia Phillies and the Cincinnati Reds, who tied for second.

___**QUESTION 102:** In 1968, the Cardinals pitching staff posted a league best 2.49 earned run average.

___**QUESTION 103:** The Cardinals scored 1,004 runs in 1930.

___**QUESTION 104:** The Cardinals hit a mere 67 home runs in 1982, en route to their ninth World Series championship.

___**QUESTION 105:** The 1985 Cardinals racked up 304 stolen bases.

THE ROOKIES

___QUESTION 106: The four Cardinal outfielders to win Rookie of the Year awards: Wally Moon, Bill Virdon, Bake McBride, and Vince Coleman.

___QUESTION 107: George Watkins hit .373 for the Cards in his rookie year of 1930.

___QUESTION 108: Vince Coleman was the rookie brought up in 1985 to fill in for the injured Willie McGee; he never returned to the minors even after McGee got healthy.

___QUESTION 109: Willie McGee was the rookie brought up in 1982 to fill in for the injured David Green; he never returned to the minors even after Green got healthy.

___QUESTION 110: Willie McGee was the rookie Howard Cosell proclaimed looked like E.T.

THE VETERANS

___QUESTION 111: Grover Cleveland Alexander's last Major League win came with the Cardinals in 1929.

___QUESTION 112: In Roger Maris' last regular season at bat in 1968, he hit a long fly ball down the right field line at Busch Stadium, which missed going out of the park by a matter of inches; by the time Maris started running (after the ball hit the wall) he wound up with a triple, instead of an easy inside-the-park home run.

___**QUESTION 113:** Jim Kaat came over to the Cardinals from the Twins in 1980, and his prowess helped the Redbirds capture the 1982 world championship.

___**QUESTION 114:** Burleigh Grimes had that nickname.

___**QUESTION 115:** Moe Drabowski surrendered Musial's 3,000th hit in 1958 before joining the Cardinals in the early '70s.

THE LEGENDS

___**QUESTION 116:** One of the greatest all-around athletes to play baseball, Bob Gibson played for the Harlem Globetrotters before signing with the Cardinals.

___**QUESTION 117:** For some reason, Alexander's nickname was "Pete."

___**QUESTION 118:** The only "All-Brother" All-Star battery in Major League history was Mort and Walker Cooper, in 1942.

___**QUESTION 119:** Hornsby won seven batting titles during his career (six in a row).

___**QUESTION 120:** In 1963, the entire starting infield in the All-Star Game was comprised of Cardinals: Bill White, Julian Javier, Ken Boyer, and Dick Groat.

THE HITTERS

___**QUESTION 121:** Joe Medwick's 64 doubles in 1936 is still a NL record.

___**QUESTION 122:** Albert Pujols hit the first home run for the Cardinals in Game 1 of the 2006 World Series.

___**QUESTION 123:** Mark McGwire's 62nd home run of the season was a shot that barely cleared the left field wall down the line, traveling a little over 340 feet.

___**QUESTION 124:** Vince Coleman's first career home run was a shot down the right field line which bounced high off the wall and caromed away from the outfielders, as he scored without a play at the plate.

___**QUESTION 125:** Musial had a great day, but the Cards and Giants split the doubleheader.

THE PITCHERS

___QUESTION 126: Bruce Sutter recorded 45 saves in 1984, and left the Cardinals as a free agent after compiling his record setting total.

___QUESTION 127: Nelson Briles won the pivotal Game 3 of the 1967 World Series for the Cardinals; the only game not won by Bob Gibson for the Redbirds.

___QUESTION 128: Old Grover Alexander won 21 games for the Cardinals in 1927, at the tender age of 40.

___QUESTION 129: The good-natured Canadian, Reggie Cleveland, had that portly nickname.

___QUESTION 130: Gibson was never taken out of a game while he was still on the mound in 1968.

THE MANAGERS, COACHES, ANNOUNCERS, AND TRADES

___QUESTION 131: Jack Buck was the voice of the Ohio State Buckeyes before joining the Cardinals.

___QUESTION 132: After getting fired from Cardinals in 1969, Harry Caray first went to Oakland, then to the Chicago White Sox before gaining fame as a Cubs announcer.

___**QUESTION 133:** The Cards got pitcher Rick Wise from Philadelphia, in exchange for Steve Carlton.

___**QUESTION 134:** Light hitting Jose Oquendo's surprise three-run homer gave the Cardinals all the runs they needed to beat San Francisco.

___**QUESTION 135:** Ray Jablonski drove in over 100 runs in his first two seasons with the Cardinals, but his poor fielding at third base hastened his departure.

THE FABULOUS FEATS

___**QUESTION 136:** "Hard Hittin'" Mark Whiten stroked four home runs while driving in 12 against the Cincinnati Reds in 1992.

___**QUESTION 137:** Cardinals great Jim Bottomley was the first player in Major League history to drive in 12 runs in a single game.

___**QUESTION 138:** Willie McGee hit for the cycle, but Ryne Sandberg was the star of the game for the Cubs, hitting a couple of home runs off none other than Cards relief ace, Bruce Sutter; the last one being a game-winner.

___**QUESTION 139:** On September 15, 1986, Mike Laga swung a bit early, crushing a long foul ball completely out of Busch Stadium; the only player to do it in the history of the ballpark. Of course, the

Cards fans gave him a standing ovation after his fabulous feat.

___QUESTION 140: Bobby Bonds still had good wheels in 1980, and scooted home from first base on a double down the left field line, giving the Cardinals an Opening Day victory against Pittsburgh.

THE TEAMS

___QUESTION 141: After McGwire's 70 home runs, the Cardinals had three other players hitting at least 25: Ray Lankford (31), Ron Gant (26), and Brian Jordan (25).

___QUESTION 142: In 1974, Lou Brock, Bake McBride, and Reggie Smith all hit over .300 for the Cardinals.

___QUESTION 143: Hector Cruz was not only a terrible fielder, he didn't hit much either for the Cardinals in 1976.

___QUESTION 144: The 1986 Cardinals were the last team to hit fewer than 60 home runs in a single season.

___QUESTION 145: In both 1973 and 1974, the Cards finished just a game and a half behind division winners, the New York Mets and Pittsburgh Pirates, respectively.

MISCELLANEOUS

___**QUESTION 146:** False. Pujols only scored 99 runs in 2007.

___**QUESTION 147:** True. Pujols has driven in at least 100 runs in every season he's played.

___**QUESTION 148:** True. Pujols currently has a .334 lifetime batting average; Musial's was .331.

___**QUESTION 149:** Leo Durocher was appropriately given that nickname.

___**QUESTION 150:** Bob Forsch and Tommy Herr were the only players to play on both the 1980 and 1987 Cardinals.

Got your All-Star total? Here's how it breaks down:

LEADING VOTE GETTER & GAME MVP	= 45-50
WON THE HOME RUN DERBY	= 40-44
MADE THE TEAM ON THE FINAL FAN VOTE	= 35-39
NOT QUITE ALL-STAR MATERIAL	= 30-34
SORRY, NO CIGAR!	= 00-29

Time to regroup and get ready for the stretch run—clutch up!

Chapter Four

DOG DAYS OF SUMMER

AH, THE HEAT, THE HUMIDITY ... just like St. Louis weather, the season is heating up now. The Mid-Summer Classic is behind us, the trade deadline is rapidly approaching, and the race for the postseason is in full throttle.

It's the Dog Days of Summer.

This is when the cagey veterans make their presence known, the weak begin to fade from contention, and that rare breed of player who just plain knows how to win – or who refuses to lose – achieves baseball immortality with his clutch exploits on the field, at the time of year when every action is magnified, and when his team and its fans need him the absolute most. Think you're that kind of player? We're about to find out ... it's the Dog Days.

THE NUMBERS GAME

QUESTION 151: Who holds the Cardinals franchise record for most RBIs in a single season, how many did he tally, and in what year did he accomplish this?

QUESTION 152: Name the first Cardinals player to drive in over 150 runs in a single season, and in what year did he do it?

QUESTION 153: Whose seven RBIs led the Cardinals in the 1967 World Series?

QUESTION 154: How many times did Stan Musial drive in 100 runs?

QUESTION 155: Who was the first Cardinals player to lead the league in stolen bases three different times?

THE ROOKIES

QUESTION 156: Who won Rookie of the Year honors after he appeared in a World Series for the Cardinals?

QUESTION 157: Who was the rookie to become the first Cardinals player since 1900 to steal at least 20 bases in fewer than 70 games?

QUESTION 158: Who was the rookie left-handed pitcher to lead the NL in walks in 1952?

QUESTION 159: This 20-year-old rookie catcher became the youngest player in Cardinals history to catch in as many as 50 games in a season. Who was he?

QUESTION 160: Who is the only player to win Rookie of the Year honors on a Cardinals pennant-winner?

THE VETERANS

QUESTION 161: What career milestones did Joe Torre reach while with the Cardinals in 1973?

QUESTION 162: Name the player who led the 1934 Gas House Gang in batting, home runs and RBIs.

QUESTION 163: True or False. The 1931 World Champion Cardinals had just one player with 20 home runs and 100 RBIs that season.

QUESTION 164: Who pitched a three-hit shutout against Atlanta in Game 1 of the 1982 NLCS?

QUESTION 165: True or False. Stan Musial only hit 40 home runs in a season one time in his career.

THE LEGENDS

QUESTION 166: Who led the NL with a .349 batting average in 1931?

QUESTION 167: Whose nickname was "Country?"

QUESTION 168: Who had ten straight hits during the 1936 season?

QUESTION 169: Who recorded the highest single season batting average for a NL switch-hitter?

QUESTION 170: What Cardinal outfielder led the NL in putouts with a perfect 1.000 fielding average in 1966?

THE HITTERS

QUESTION 171: What three Cardinal MVPs later played for the Mets?

QUESTION 172: Who holds the NL record for most total bases in a single season?

QUESTION 173: Who led the Cardinals with a .335 batting average in 1967?

QUESTION 174: Who broke up Jim Lonborg's no-hit bid in Game 2 of the 1967 World Series?

QUESTION 175: Name the MVP who hit .363 with 230 hits and 137 RBIs.

THE PITCHERS

QUESTION 176: Who was the left-hander that shut out the Dodgers five times in 1966?

QUESTION 177: The day after Gaylord Perry no-hit the Cardinals in 1968, who came back to no-hit the Giants?

QUESTION 178: Who went 18-9 for the '64 Cardinals?

QUESTION 179: Who was the only pitcher with a losing record and an earned run average over 3.00 with the Cards in 1968?

QUESTION 180: Who led the Cardinals with 222 innings pitched in 1967?

THE MANAGERS, COACHES, ANNOUNCERS, AND TRADES

QUESTION 181: Who coined the rallying cry, "The Cardinals are coming, tra-la-la-la?"

QUESTION 182: When the Cardinals won 105 regular season games in 2004, what World Series occurrence made history when they later squared off against Boston?

QUESTION 183: Name the only Cardinals manager to win a World Series championship who never played in the Major Leagues.

QUESTION 184: Who is the only manager in team history to lead the Cards to winning seasons in each of his first three years at the helm?

QUESTION 185: Who managed the Cardinals during Lou Brock's final season?

THE FABULOUS FEATS

QUESTION 186: Who is the only Cardinal to steal five bases in a single game?

QUESTION 187: Name the first position player in ML history to wear glasses, and what year did that happen?

QUESTION 188: Name the only NL pitcher to hit into an unassisted triple play in regular season play. When did he do it, and who victimized him?

QUESTION 189: Name the first pinch-hitter in ML history to have as many as four pinch home runs in consecutive seasons, and what years did he accomplish the feats?

QUESTION 190: Who pitched two one-hitters and two two-hitters among his nine wins in 1978?

THE TEAMS

QUESTION 191: The Cardinals won pennants in 1926 and 1928; how close were they to winning the pennant in 1927?

QUESTION 192: What was the first team in ML history to finish under .500 the year after winning the World Series?

QUESTION 193: The Cardinals led the NL with 27 home runs in 1918; where did they finish in the standings that year?

QUESTION 194: During the '60s, the Cardinals, Dodgers, and Giants were the three most successful teams in the NL. In terms of total victories for the decade, how did the three teams rank?

QUESTION 195: The Cardinals won four NL pennants and three World Series championships in the 1940s; how many times did they finish second during the decade?

MISCELLANEOUS

QUESTION 196: The Cardinals didn't waste any time to have a no-hitter thrown at them in the 20th century—it happened in 1901. Who was the pitcher that baffled them?

QUESTION 197: In 1984 what Cardinals pitcher hit home runs batting both right and left-handed?

QUESTION 198: In how many All-Star Games did Stan Musial play?

QUESTION 199: Who scored the winning run for the Cardinals in the longest extra-inning game they ever played?

QUESTION 200: Who led all Major League outfielders by throwing out 20 runners in 1979?

Chapter Four Answer Key

Time to find out how you did – put a check mark next to the questions you answered correctly, and when you're done be sure to add up your score to find out your IQ, and most importantly, how you did down the stretch. Hot enough for you?

THE NUMBERS GAME

___**QUESTION 151:** Joe Medwick – 154, 1937.

___**QUESTION 152:** Rogers Hornsby in 1922.

___**QUESTION 153:** Roger Maris, who also hit .385.

___**QUESTION 154:** Stan the Man knocked in at least 100 in ten different seasons.

___**QUESTION 155:** Pepper Martin did it before Lou Brock came along.

THE ROOKIES

___**QUESTION 156:** Todd Worrell joined the Cards in '85 and saw World Series action, then won the NL Rookie of the Year award in '86.

___**QUESTION 157:** Terry Pendleton did the trick in 1984.

___**QUESTION 158:** "Vinegar Bend" Mizell, who also had a great nickname.

___**QUESTION 159:** It was St. Louis native Joe Garagiola, who joined the Cards in 1946.

___**QUESTION 160:** Vince Coleman did it in 1985.

THE VETERANS

___**QUESTION 161:** Joe reached the 2,000 hits and 1,000 RBIs plateaus that season.

___**QUESTION 162:** "Ripper" Collins. He also led the team in slugging, hits, runs, and total bases!

___**QUESTION 163:** False. Nobody hit 20 home runs and nobody drove in at least 100 that year.

___**QUESTION 164:** Bob Forsch was the pitching hero for the Redbirds in that game.

___**QUESTION 165:** False. Stan the Man's highest home run total in any season was 39 (1948).

THE LEGENDS

___**QUESTION 166:** "Chick" Hafey; for some reason, he was traded by the next season.

___**QUESTION 167:** Enos Slaughter.

___**QUESTION 168:** Joe Medwick.

___**QUESTION 169:** Willie McGee did it, with a .353 mark in 1985.

___**QUESTION 170:** Curt Flood.

THE HITTERS

___**QUESTION 171:** Ken Boyer, Joe Torre, and Keith Hernandez.

___**QUESTION 172:** Rogers Hornsby tallied 450 total bases in 1922, a NL record.

___**QUESTION 173:** Curt Flood was ten points higher than MVP Orlando Cepeda.

___**QUESTION 174:** Julian Javier did it with a double down the left field line; it was the only hit of the game for the Cardinals.

___**QUESTION 175:** Joe Torre posted those memorable stats in 1971.

THE PITCHERS

___**QUESTION 176:** Larry Jaster; his five shutouts of the Dodgers were the only ones he threw all season. It was still enough to lead the NL.

___**QUESTION 177:** Ray Washburn evened the no-hit score the very next day at Candlestick Park.

___**QUESTION 178:** Curt Simmons. His 18 wins was a career high.

___**QUESTION 179:** Larry Jaster. He went 9-13 with a 3.51 ERA.

___**QUESTION 180:** Dick Hughes.

THE MANAGERS, COACHES, ANNOUNCERS, AND TRADES

___**QUESTION 181:** That was Harry Caray's late season brainchild in 1969. It didn't work. The Cards didn't win and Harry was fired after the season ended.

___**QUESTION 182:** They became the first NL team to win that many regular season games and be swept in a World Series.

___**QUESTION 183:** Johnny Keane, 1964.

___**QUESTION 184:** Joe Torre did it from 1991-93. He was rewarded for his efforts by getting fired.

___**QUESTION 185:** Ken Boyer.

THE FABULOUS FEATS

___QUESTION 186: Lonnie Smith did it in 1982.

___QUESTION 187: George "Specs" Toporcer did it way back in 1921.

___QUESTION 188: Woody Williams got the green light, the runners were off, but Rafael Furcal got in the way of that line drive in 2003.

___QUESTION 189: George Crowe was the first player in ML history to have as many as four pinch home runs in two consecutive seasons. He did it in 1959 and 1960.

___QUESTION 190: Silvio Martinez.

THE TEAMS

___QUESTION 191: The 1927 Cardinals finished in second place, a game and a half behind the Pittsburgh Pirates.

___QUESTION 192: The Cardinals went 80-81 in 1965.

___QUESTION 193: They finished last; eighth place.

___QUESTION 194: (1) Giants, 902 wins; (2) Cardinals, 884 wins; (3) Dodgers, 878 wins.

___**QUESTION 195:** The Cardinals finished second in the NL five times during the '40s.

MISCELLANEOUS

___**QUESTION 196:** Christy Mathewson tossed that no-hitter – no slouch!

___**QUESTION 197:** Joaquin Andujar decided to become a switch hitter that year – he was pretty successful from a power perspective!

___**QUESTION 198:** "Stan the Man" played in 24 All-Star Games during his career.

___**QUESTION 199:** On September 11, 1974, Bake McBride scored all the way from first base on a wild pickoff throw in the 25th inning, to help the Cards win the marathon game against the Mets at Shea Stadium.

___**QUESTION 200:** George Hendrick let his strong right arm do the talking for him!

Got your Dog Days total? Here's how it breaks down:

WON PENNANT AND NLCS MVP HONORS	= 45-50
WON PENNANT IN SEVEN-GAME SERIES	= 40-44
DIVISION CHAMPION	= 35-39
HUNG IN THERE FOR THE WILD CARD	= 30-34
AT HOME WATCHING ON TV	= 00-29

Good luck in October! Hit 'em where they ain't!

Chapter Five

OCTOBER BASEBALL

IT ALL COMES DOWN TO THIS. You spent your childhood dreaming of this moment.

It's October baseball.

This is your chance at baseball immortality. You're the underdog. No one expected you to make it this far, but at least to this point you've proved everyone wrong. The only thing left to prove is that you have what it takes to be a world champion. No need to be nervous – it's not like we saved the 50 toughest questions for last for anything!

THE NUMBERS GAME

QUESTION 201: Who was the first Cardinals player to hit at least 20 home runs for three consecutive seasons?

QUESTION 202: Whose number do you get when you take Whitey Herzog's number, subtract Ted Simmons' number, add Stan Musial's number, and then subtract Red Schoendienst's number?

QUESTION 203: Which player led the Cardinals in hits in 1959, and was rewarded for his efforts by being traded in 1960?

QUESTION 204: Which player led the NL with 43 doubles in 1963, along with collecting 201 hits for the year?

QUESTION 205: Who led the NL with 282 innings pitched in 1960?

THE ROOKIES

QUESTION 206: Name the only Cardinals rookie pitcher to win 20 games on a pennant-winning team.

QUESTION 207: Which slugger led NL rookies with eight home runs, while playing in just 97 games for the Cardinals?

QUESTION 208: Which rookie topped the NL with 18 wins for the Cardinals, and after a short-lived career went on to be a NL umpire for many years?

QUESTION 209: This versatile player set a Cardinals record for hitting safely in 25 consecutive games as a rookie. Who was he?

QUESTION 210: This left-hander posted a team leading 13 saves as a rookie, with an impressive 1.54 ERA in 57 appearances; who was he?

THE VETERANS

QUESTION 211: This former Giants slugger was a key late-season acquisition for the Cardinals, helping them reach the postseason with his clutch hitting. He retired at the end of that season. Who was he?

QUESTION 212: Who collected his 999th and final hit playing for the Cardinals before retiring?

QUESTION 213: What former Cubs All-Star shortstop had a brief stint (1976-77) with the Cardinals when he was just about washed up as a player?

QUESTION 214: Which player spent two seasons with the Cardinals, before retiring with 275 career home runs?

QUESTION 215: What player was traded after hitting .200 for the Cardinals in ten games, and wound up winning the NL batting title with his new team?

THE LEGENDS

QUESTION 216: Who managed the Cardinals the year before they won their first World Series championship in 1926?

QUESTION 217: How was the last out recorded in the 1926 World Series?

QUESTION 218: How was the last out recorded in the 1982 World Series?

QUESTION 219: Who scored from second base on a sacrifice fly in the 1982 World Series?

QUESTION 220: How was the last out recorded when Bob Gibson threw his only no-hitter against the Pirates in 1971?

THE HITTERS

QUESTION 221: What Cardinals player collected over 200 hits while hitting under .300 for a team that went on to win the World Series?

QUESTION 222: Between Stan Musial in 1952 and Albert Pujols in 2003, name the only other Cardinals player to lead the NL in total bases.

QUESTION 223: Prior to Albert Pujols, who was the last Cardinals player to have three consecutive 100 RBI seasons while hitting over .300 each year?

QUESTION 224: What player posted the most RBIs in a season since World War II without hitting a single home run?

QUESTION 225: What member of the Gas House Gang set the current Cards record for most RBIs by a switch-hitter?

THE PITCHERS

QUESTION 226: Who posted the highest ERA for any Cy Young award winner?

QUESTION 227: Who was the first pitcher in NL history to have three consecutive seasons with 40 or more saves, and when did he accomplish that feat?

QUESTION 228: Aside from Bob Gibson, who was the last Cardinals pitcher to win at least 20 games in back-to-back seasons?

QUESTION 229: In 1980, who pitched an extra-inning shutout for the Cardinals at the age of 41?

QUESTION 230: How many consecutive games did Bob Gibson win in 1968?

THE MANAGERS, COACHES, ANNOUNCERS, AND TRADES

QUESTION 231: The Cardinals had one manager per year from 1950-52. Name them.

QUESTION 232: Who did the Cardinals receive in the trade that sent pitcher Eric Rasmussen to the San Diego Padres?

QUESTION 233: Who did the Cardinals dispatch to the Pittsburgh Pirates in exchange for pitcher John Tudor in 1985?

QUESTION 234: Who did the Cardinals receive in the trade that sent Willie McGee to the Oakland A's in 1990?

QUESTION 235: Who did the Cardinals send to the Kansas City Royals in exchange for Gregg Jeffries in 1993?

THE FABULOUS FEATS

QUESTION 236: Twenty Cardinals have hit for the cycle in franchise history. Who was the most recent player to do it?

QUESTION 237: Who led the NL with a 2.18 ERA in 1988?

QUESTION 238: Who was the slick fielding second baseman that established a ML record in 1990 by only committing three errors all season?

QUESTION 239: It should come as no surprise that Ozzie Smith holds the Major League record for fewest errors committed by a shortstop; what season did he accomplish the feat, and how many errors was he charged with?

QUESTION 240: What is the Cardinals team record for most strikeouts by the pitching staff in a single season, and when did they accomplish this feat?

THE TEAMS

QUESTION 241: When was the last time the Cardinals had two 20-game winners in the same season, and who were the hurlers that did the trick?

QUESTION 242: When was the last time any NL club had three players with at least 200 hits in a season, and who were the three players to do it?

QUESTION 243: When was the last time the Cardinals posted a team ERA under 3.00?

QUESTION 244: In what year did the Cardinals draw one million fans for the first time?

QUESTION 245: In what year did the Cardinals draw three million fans for the first time?

MISCELLANEOUS

QUESTION 246: What was Mike Shannon's nickname?

QUESTION 247: Name the Cardinals outfielder who also was a very talented artist. He even painted team owner Gussie Busch's portrait.

QUESTION 248: Name the Dodgers pitcher who gave up the big home runs to Ozzie Smith and Jack Clark in the 1985 NLCS.

QUESTION 249: Name the batter who lined a shot off Dizzy Dean's big toe in the 1937 All-Star Game, an injury which hastened the premature end of Dean's career.

QUESTION 250: What was Jim Bottomley's most appropriate nickname?

Chapter Five Answer Key

Time to find out how you did – put a check mark next to the questions you answered correctly, and when you're done be sure to add up your score to find out your IQ and whether or not you've earned a world championship ring!

THE NUMBERS GAME

___QUESTION 201: Chick Hafey, from 1928-30.

___QUESTION 202: 24-23+6-2 = 5. That's Albert Pujols' number, but you already knew that.

___QUESTION 203: Don Blasingame.

___QUESTION 204: Dick Groat.

___QUESTION 205: Larry Jackson.

THE ROOKIES

___QUESTION 206: Johnny Beazley, 1942.

___QUESTION 207: Leon Durham, 1980.

___QUESTION 208: Ken Burkhardt, 1945.

___QUESTION 209: Joe McEwing, 1999.

___QUESTION 210: Joe Hoerner, 1966.

THE VETERANS

___QUESTION 211: Will Clark, 2000.

___QUESTION 212: Tommie Agee, 1973.

___QUESTION 213: Don Kessinger.

___QUESTION 214: Roger Maris, 1967-68.

___QUESTION 215: Harry Walker, who hit a league leading .363 in 1947; .371 as a member of the Philadelphia Phillies.

THE LEGENDS

___QUESTION 216: Branch Rickey; who proved to be a much better front office executive than manager.

___QUESTION 217: Babe Ruth, who was representing the tying run, was easily thrown out trying to steal second base.

___QUESTION 218: Bruce Sutter struck out Gorman Thomas.

___QUESTION 219: Ozzie Smith raced all the way around from second base when centerfielder

Gorman Thomas slipped as he caught the fly ball, allowing Smith to beat the relay.

___QUESTION 220: Gibson struck out Pittsburgh slugger Willie Stargell to end it with a flourish.

THE HITTERS

___QUESTION 221: Lou Brock hit .299 while stroking 206 hits in 689 at bats in 1967.

___QUESTION 222: Joe Torre with 352 in 1971.

___QUESTION 223: Bill White, 1962-64.

___QUESTION 224: Ozzie Smith plated 75 runners in 1987 with zero homers.

___QUESTION 225: Ripper Collins with 128 in 1934.

THE PITCHERS

___QUESTION 226: Just two years after his amazing 1.12 ERA, Bob Gibson bagged another Cy Young award in 1970 with an ERA exactly two runs higher – 3.12!

___QUESTION 227: Big Lee Smith did it from 1991-93.

___QUESTION 228: Joaquin Andujar won 20 games in 1984 and 1985.

___QUESTION 229: Jim Kaat.

___QUESTION 230: After a bit of a slow start, "Gibby" reeled off 15 straight wins in '68.

THE MANAGERS, COACHES, ANNOUNCERS, AND TRADES

___QUESTION 231: Eddie Dyer (1950), Marty Marion (1951), and Eddie Stanky (1952).

___QUESTION 232: George Hendrick, 1978.

___QUESTION 233: It was George Hendrick again.

___QUESTION 234: Felix Jose.

___QUESTION 235: It was Felix Jose, of course.

THE FABULOUS FEATS

___QUESTION 236: Mark Grudzielanek did it in 2005.

___QUESTION 237: Joe Magrane did it, but somehow only managed to win the grand total of five games that year.

___QUESTION 238: Jose Oquendo pulled off that remarkable fielding gem.

___**QUESTION 239:** The "Wizard of Oz" only made eight errors all season in 1991.

___**QUESTION 240:** In 1996, the staff racked up 1,050 strikeouts – a new team record.

THE TEAMS

___**QUESTION 241:** John Tudor and Joaquin Andujar did it in 1985.

___**QUESTION 242:** In 1963, Curt Flood, Dick Groat, and Bill White all had at least 200 hits for the second place Cardinals.

___**QUESTION 243:** They did it in 1969, but still finished 13 games behind the Mets in the NL Eastern Division race.

___**QUESTION 244:** They first did it in the world championship season of 1946.

___**QUESTION 245:** They first did it in the pennant-winning season of 1987.

MISCELLANEOUS

___**QUESTION 246:** He was known as "Shannon the Cannon" in certain circles, but Mike Shannon's most celebrated nickname was "Moon Man."

___QUESTION 247: Curt Flood was not only a magician with the glove; he handled a paintbrush with a great deal of aplomb as well.

___QUESTION 248: Tom Niedenfuer was victimized by Ozzie in Game 5 and then by Jack "The Ripper" Clark in the deciding Game 6.

___QUESTION 249: Future Hall of Fame outfielder Earl Averill was a terrific line drive hitter for the Cleveland Indians, and Dizzy Dean probably wished he never faced him.

___QUESTION 250: He always had a smile on his face, and he loved to play baseball, hence his nickname "Sunny Jim."

Got your October total? Here's how it breaks down:

WALK-OFF BOMB WON GAME 7	= 45-50
WON A THRILLING SEVEN-GAME SERIES	= 40-44
YOU DID ENOUGH TO GET THE RING	= 35-39
LOST A TOUGH SEVEN-GAME SERIES	= 30-34
HITLESS IN A FOUR-GAME SWEEP	= 00-29

Think you can do better next season? Well, you're going to get a shot at it—St. Louis Cardinals IQ Volume II is coming in 2011!

About the Author

LARRY UNDERWOOD GREW UP IN ST. LOUIS and has been following the Cardinals for over 50 years. He 's a retired executive who recently published a book about his 26-year career with the car rental giant, Enterprise; *Life Under the Corporate Microscope – A Maverick's Irreverent Perspective.* This is his second book.

References

Broeg, Bob, *Super Stars of Baseball* (St. Louis: The Sporting News, 1971).

Buck, Jack and Rains, Rob *"That's a Winner!"* (Champaign IL: Sagamore Publishing, 1997).

Devine, Bing and Wheatley, Tom, *The Memoirs of Bing Devine – Stealing Lou Brock and Other Winning Moves by a Master Gm* (USA: Sports Publishing, LLC, 2004).

Getz, Mike, *St. Louis Cardinals Trivia* (Boston: Quinlan Press, 1987).

Gibson, Bob and Wheeler, Lonnie, *Stranger to the Game – The Autobiography of Bob Gibson* (New York: Penguin Books, 1994).

Golenbock, Peter, *The Spirit of St. Louis – A History of the St. Louis Cardinals and Browns* (New York: Avon Books, Inc, 2000).

Lansche, Jerry, *Stan the Man Musial – Born to Be a Ballplayer* (Dallas: Taylor Publishing Company, 1994).

McCarver, Tim and Pepe, Phil, *Few and Chosen –*
    Defining Cardinal Greatness Across the Eras
    (Chicago: Triumph Books, 2003).

Nemec, David and Flatow, Scott, *This Day in*
    Baseball – A Day-by-Day Record of the
    Events That Shaped the Game (Lanham MD:
    Taylor Trade Publishing, 2009).

Nemec, David and Flatow, Scott, *Ultimate St. Louis*
    Cardinals Baseball Challenge (Lanham MD:
    Taylor Trade Publishing, 2008).

Rains, Rob, *St. Louis Cardinals – 100th Anniversary –*
    1892-1992 (New York: St Martin's Press,
    1992).

Reichler, Joseph, *The Baseball Encyclopedia – The*
    Complete and Official Record of Major
    League Baseball (New York: MacMillan
    Publishing Co, Inc, 1979).

Smith, Ozzie and Rains, Rob, *Wizard* (Chicago:
    Contemporary Books, 1988).

Websites

MLB.com
StLouis.Cardinals.MLB.com

Baseball-reference.com

About Black Mesa

Look for these other titles in the IQ Series:

- *Mixed Martial Arts (Volumes I & II)*
- *New York Yankees*
- *Atlanta Braves*
- *Boston Red Sox (Volumes I & II)*
- *Milwaukee Brewers*
- *Tampa Bay Rays*
- *Kansas City Royals*
- *Cincinnati Reds*
- *Major League Baseball*
- *Boston Celtics*
- *New England Patriots*
- *University of Texas Longhorns Football*
- *University of Oklahoma Sooners Football*
- *University of Florida Gators Football*
- *University of Georgia Bulldogs Football*

For information about special discounts for bulk purchases, please email:

black.mesa.publishing@gmail.com

www.blackmesabooks.com

Sports by the Numbers

- *Major League Baseball*
- *New York Yankees*
- *Boston Red Sox*
- *San Francisco Giants*
- *University of Oklahoma Football*
- *University of Georgia Football*
- *Penn State University Football*
- *NASCAR*
- *Sacramento Kings Basketball*
- *Mixed Martial Arts*

Available Soon from Black Mesa

- *Texas Rangers*
- *Los Angeles Dodgers*
- *Boston Celtics*
- *Dallas Cowboys*

16756035R00057

Made in the USA
Middletown, DE
20 December 2014